GIULIO MARINI

florence
art and life

108 Colour Plates

MEDIEVAL FLORENCE

Like many other Italian cities, Florence was born in very far-off days, on the banks of a river (the Arno) at a point where its course narrows, making possible a ford (where to-day is the Old Bridge) (Ponte Vecchio). The nucleus emanated from nearby Fiesole in a position of defence on the hills. The presence of the Etruscans in VII Cent. B. C. is evidenced by findings in the necropolises, but it was the Romans, always in search of suitable road-crossings who determined its importance. First a municipality, later a colony, founded by the veterans of Caesar's army, the new city known as Florentia, grew rapidly following the normal scheme of such camps. Observing the area of the city of to-day comprised between the two Squares of the Cathedral and the Signoria, the Arno and Via Tornabuoni, the squared network of the Roman street system is still evident, with the Forum corresponding to the Piazza della Repubblica. In the imperial era the architecture of the city must have assumed grandiose forms, but no documentations remain save the knowledge that the Theatre was on a site near the Piazza della Signoria, the Baths where nowadays is the Via delle Terme (Baths), the Amphitheatre outside the walls, near the square of Santa Croce (Holy Cross) where, much later, were built the houses of the Peruzzi with their curved façades.

Above the Roman nucleus, placed on the right hand bank of the river, were superimposed the medieval and Renaissance cities, spreading like oil stains on both banks.

The birth of Florentine power goes back to the XI Cent. It, too, participated in the history of Italy, centred on the discord between the two greatest medieval institutions, the Papacy and the Empire. In the first years of the XI Cent. the entire Tuscan March was governed by the Marquis Hugo in the name of the Emperor; in the second half of the same century Pope Gregory VII found a powerful ally in the famous Countess Matilda of Canossa. The religious fervour of Florence at that time is evidenced by the flourishing of numerous religious edifices: churches and monasteries were re-built or founded inside and outside the circle of walls, also renewed on the ancient Roman outline. The Romanesque architecture of this period, even though on the common matrix of Italian art, reveals stylistic motifs differentiated by a greater solidity and linearity of clear Roman derivation.

Towards the end of the XII Cent. Florence had achieved its effective communal autonomy. The most evident social phenomenon was the immigration of the rural population from the country towards the city.

Even the nobles, the ancient feudatories who, from their towered castles dictated the law to the city, were forced to live in the city, whither they took all their political passions, personal hatreds and antagonisms, but also the money accumulated in precedence. They built mansions and fortress-like houses and vied with one another in raising the highest or best fortified towers. Later when the power of this ruling class was decisively on the wane and other social classes acquired power and prestige, the fortress-houses and towers were torn down and demolished. Even the form of government was no longer of the noble type but assumed, rather, an associative character

s of Badia and of Palazzo della Signoria

with the participation of the lesser vassals, the great merchants, joined later by the lower orders of the population, such as small land-owners, tradesmen, artisans, shop-keepers, and those people, too, organized in guilds according to their trade. Even the episcopal authority, in its political sense, disappeared, though the Commune had drawn up the first public acts in its name, in the effort to avenge itself upon its former master, that is to say, the Empire. Having acquired complete autonomy, Florence was governed by its own men and magistrates known as Consuls, who were elected for a temporary term of office. Later, to maintain peace and internal justice, they resorted to the institution of a local Podestà; finally, in 1200, to a Podestà from another city. In Tuscany, other cities had attained a certain autonomy and wealth before Florence, among them Pisa, because of its privileged position on the sea, then Siena, Lucca, Arezzo. Florence, while last to enter the communal lists, knew well how to impose its greater force of character and will to emerge. The new ruling class, made up of merchants who had got rich the hard way, needed freedom of movement to increase commerce and earnings. Roads and

Cenacle of S. Apollonia. Andrea del Castagno: Dante (portrait)

Via Dante Alighieri

4

rivers must be safe, the Customs instituted by every city to protect its own products must go. The history of Florence is, above all, one of internal strife, its politics among the most turbulent for the violence and passions with which the factions contested power. War between classes, armed one against the other, temporarily interested allies. Hence the repeated discord between the two parties then dividing all Italy between them, Guelphs, partisans of the Pope, Ghibellines, supporters of the Emperor. From the beginning Florence was Guelph because the nobles surrounding and threatening it were Ghibellines, vassals invested with their fiefs and privileges by the Emperors. The Ghibellines, chased out of the city, had long schemed to return; they were allied with Siena and finally, in 1260, defeated the Guelphs at Montaperti. Every upheaval meant the extermination or exile of the losing side, and this time too the Ghibellines hastened to put into practice this violent means of retaliation. But the victory was of short duration, the invasion of Italy by Charles of Anjou, new King of Naples, and the battles of Benevento and Tagliacozzo struck a final blow at Ghibellines and supporters, too. In Tuscany, following the

ia dei Cerchi

Cenacle of S. Apollonia. Andrea del Castagno:
Farinata degli Uberti (portrait)

Palazzo della Signoria. Loggia della Signoria

slow decline of Pisa, Florence overcame, one after the other, Lucca, Pistoia and finally, in 1289, Arezzo the last stronghold of the Ghibellines. The Florentines were now freer to devote themselves to their industries, their commerce and banking. This last was among the most profitable activities of the city, known all over Europe, and to which many noblemen and monarchs had recourse for loans. The banking systems introduced by Florence, letters of exchange or credit, speeded up the forms of exchange and increased perceptibly the commerce not only of Florence itself, but of all Europe. Not that this caused any diminution in the intensity of intestine strife and discord. At times it seems incredible that the Florentines, in the midst of these continuous upheavals were able to develop economically, socially and culturally at so high a level.

Comparing the area occupied by the city in Roman days, Florence appears already to have doubled itself by 1172. Urban development in the second half of the XIII Cent. right up to the first 20 years of the next, is even more intense, so that, within its new circle of walls, the city presents an area roughly five times as large as within the earlier walls. It is now a great industrial metropolis, eager to equal Milan in the race for supremacy in Italy.

The population continues to grow, arriving at possibly one hundred and thirty thousand inhabitants, and equally, the standard of living becomes higher. Houses are built, many mansions, sumptuous dwellings, new churches and monasteries. Industries continue to increase, wool is worked in more than two hundred shops employing over thirty thousand workers, minor industries are also growing. The volume of business is enormous, supported by a capitalistic regime that works well. Dress becomes more luxurious, and personal ornament and house furnishings more splendid; similarly, the love of culture increases; art, whether architecture, sculpture, painting, or literature, is becoming appreciated. The Corporations of the Arts had great importance, divided into the Greater and the Lesser Arts, and to which all citizens who wished to have a voice in the government had to belong. In the first years of the XIII Cent. the Florentines called mosaic workers from Venice to decorate the dome of the Baptistery, the religious symbol of the power and fortunes of Florence. But in the second

Dante's House

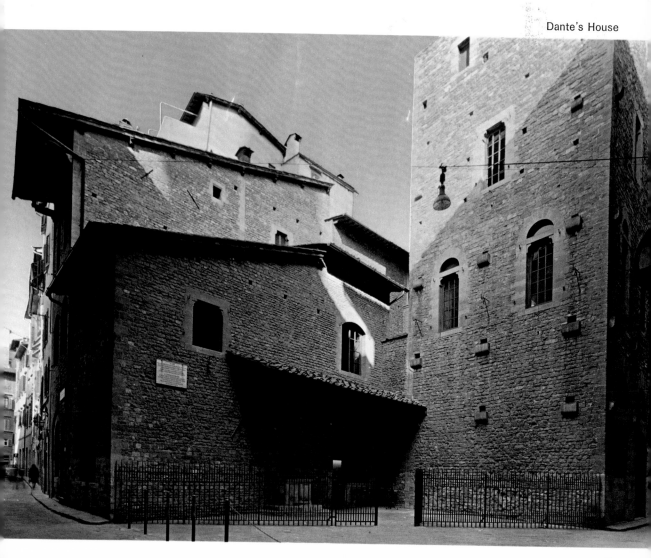

7

Uffizi Gallery. Simone Martini and Lippo Memmi: Annunciation

Gallery. Giotto di
ne: Madonna
ned and Child

half of the same century one can include local artists, first of all Cimabue, who lent a new impetus to painting, freeing it from tradition, and the architect and sculptor, Arnolfo di Cambio. And now, in this period, comes the assertion of the Florentine language, the «vulgar», over Latin, used hitherto in public documents. Brunetto Latini wrote the «Tesoretto» (Little Treasure) in «vulgar», while the literary group known under the name of «Dolce stil nuovo» (The sweet new style) asserts itself. By now we are on the threshold of that stupendous period marked by the genius of Giotto and Dante.

In 1293 Florentine government was reformed on more democratic lines with the new Codes of Justice and the appointment of the Gonfalonier of Justice supported by the Priors of the Arts and Liberty. This was a period of great prosperity which continued into the nect century, during which the city expanded and flourished in every field. The two main centres of the city emerged architectonically, the religious, with the new Cathedral in front of the Baptistery, the political with the Palazzo della Signoria. The boroughs which had continued to form outside the walls were englobed within a huge new fortified circle of walls, and inside rose other important buildings such as the Bell-tower, the Bigallo Loggia, Orsanmichele, the Bargello, the Signoria Loggia, Santa Maria Novella (St. Mary the New) and the church of Santa Croce (Holy Cross) (re-buildings).

Gothic style imposed itself on the Romanesque, but once again, the Florentine artist found expression in his own particular stylistic language, equilibrating the basic elements of the Gothic itself in a classic sense. On the vast walls of churches, which provided enormous spaces, the great Giotto (1266—1336), Taddeo Gaddi (1300—66), Puccio Capanna (1334—50), Giottino (1324—69), Bernardo Daddi (1317—50) spread their stories and legends with plastic, efficacious spirit. The Florentine language was consecrated throughout the peninsula in Dante Alighieri's Divine Comedy.

The unity of the Guelph party had, however, been progressively disintegrated by two factions formed within it, the Whites and the Blacks. The latter, favoured by the Pope's envoy, Charles of Valois, and led by the ambitious Corso Donati, finished by possessing themselves of power, casting out of the city more than 600 representatives of the adverse party, among them Dante and Boccaccio's father, who joined the exiled Ghibellines and in 1312 tried in vain to return to Florence aided by the Emperor Henry VII (who died of malaria the following year).

Another generation of artists replaced the first, Andrea di Cione, called l'Orcagna (active from 1344—68), Francesco Talenti (1300—69), Niccolò and Pietro Lamberti, Giovanni Boccaccio (1313—75), Giovanni Villani (1276—1348), Francesco Petrarca (1304—74), Agnolo Gaddi (1333—1396), Spinello Aretino (1333—1410). The great, unrepeatable Florentine season of Humanism and the Renaissance was in course of preparation.

Cathedral Museum. Trades of Mankind: Plowing

Cathedral Museum. Trades of Mankind: Navigation

...edral Museum.
...es of Mankind: Vintage and Noah Drunk

...edral Museum. Trades of Mankind: Painting

Giotto's Campanile

Palazzo Medici-Riccardi, Chapel. Benozzo Gozzoli: Procession of the Magi

The Florentine Scholars are together with the Greeks and are close-shaven. Among them are: the Pulci brothers, Marsilio Ficino and others, founders together with the Greeks of the Platonic Academy under the patronage of Cosimo the Elder

Benozzo Gozzoli (1420-1497). Painted the fresco between January 1468 and December 1469 under the rule of Piero the Gouty.

Salviati tutor of Giuliano

Giuliano brother of Lorenzo the Magnificent, was victim of the Pazzi conspiracy. He was killed in the Cathedral of S. M. del Fiore during Mass on April 26, 1478. Those involved in the plot were on the one hand Jacopo de' Pazzi, Francesco and other members of the family; on the other, Pope Sixtus IV and his nephews Girolamo and Raffaele Riario

Piero the Gouty (1416-1469) Married Lucrezia Tornabuoni and was the father of Lorenzo the Magnificent, Giuliano, Maria, Nannina and Bianca. He was lord of Florence from 1464 to his death

Lorenzo, brother of Cosimo

The Greek Scholars shown with their long beards. Among them are: Plethon, Bessarion, Argyropoulos, Chalcondylas

Lorenzo the Magnificent (1449-1492), was lord of Florence from 1469 to his death. Machiavelli wrote of him thus: «With his political acumen he made Florence the leading state in Italy and foremost in the artistic and intellectual fields

Cosimo the Elder «Pater Patriae» (1389-1464) was lord of Florence from 1434 to his death. Machiavelli wrote of him: «He was the most prudent of men; grave and courteous . . . he made himself most popular with the Florentines . . . in his mode of living he was always very simple and without ostentation . . . he had an intimate knowledge of government and State affairs»

Piazza della Signoria. Loggia della Signoria. Interior

the ancient Greek and Roman texts and codices; Lorenzo dei Medici and
Angelo Poliziano wrote verse and little poems in Latin and in «vulgar»;
Filippo Brunelleschi in architecture interpreted the forgotten message
of the ancients and brought it to life in new forms. The city was transforming itself in its most apparent aspects according to the new inter-
pretation of the values of human life; clarity, elegance, security replaced
Romanesque severity and Gothic impetus. Streets and squares were
paved, the tower-houses of the XIII Cent. and the shop-houses of the
XIV Cent. in the XV Cent. became sumptuous dwellings where architectonic
expression had its particular social meaning; the Medici, Pazzi, Pitti, Strozzi,
Rucellai mansions all present a common distributive planimetric scheme,
an almost square plan, that had at its interior an open courtyard; the
rusticated façade was still closed on ground floor but open on the upper
floors with huge double mullioned windows, while on high was a great
projecting cornice. Even religious buildings acquire new spaciousness
and design following the completely new way of conceiving religion,
free from medieval fears and superstitions; S. Lorenzo, St. Mark's, Santo
Spirito (the Holy Ghost), the Foundling Hospital, the Pazzi Chapel. It is

16

Florence's magic moment of becoming the intellectual and cultural capital of the whole world then known. Filippo Brunelleschi died in 1446; the names of the artists who with their work materialized this historic moment which has no equal in the time in any country, form a long evocative list: Michelozzo Michelozzi (1396—1472), Leon Battista Alberti (1404—72), Bernardo Rossellino (1409—64), Giuliano (1432—90) and Benedetto (1442—1497) da Maiano, Masaccio (1401—28), Beato Angelico (1387—1455), Paolo Uccello (1397—1475), Andrea del Castagno (1423—1457), Benozzo Gozzoli (1420—97), Sandro Botticelli (1444—1510). Many of the already mentioned architects were also sculptors, an artistic expression which assumed great importance as the most adequate means of the celebration of man. Lorenzo Ghiberti (1378—1455), Donatello (1382—1466), Luca (1400—82) and Andrea (1435—1525) della Robbia, Antonio Rossellino (1427—79), Desiderio da Settignano (1428—64), Andrea del Pollaiolo (1433—98), Verrocchio (1435—88).

When Lorenzo the Magnificent died in 1492, a current of opposition was forming in Florence against this type of occult dominion exercised by the Medici. Girolamo Savonarola, a Dominican friar, seized on this discontent,

Uffizi Gallery. Sandro Botticelli: Allegory of Spring

and fired the souls of the people with impassioned sermons exalting the spirit of Christian sacrifice, evoking the old morality of the Florentines which had rendered them great.

European political conditions were, however, much different at that moment. France and Spain were quarrelling and Italy was becoming their field of discord and battleground. Charles VIII entered Italy; Pietro il Fatuo, Lorenzo's son, hastened to cede to the King of France the forts between Sarzana and Leghorn, keys to the Florentine defense system, the people rebelled and restored the republican regulations. But to conduct so difficult a political game at that historic moment more was needed than the mind of a friar animated by moralizing ideas and interests contained within the city walls. The Florentines split into two factions, the followers of Savonarola called the Piagnoni, the supporters of the Medici called the Palleschi. Savonarola lost, was imprisoned, tried, hanged and burnt in the Signoria Square. The Medici returned to Florence acclaimed by the people in 1512, with the Cardinal Giovanni, Lorenzo's youngest son, who the following year rose to pontifical level with the name of Leo X. He regarded Florence and Tuscany as a personal fief and as such disposed

Cathedral of S. Maria del Fiore with Campanile and Baptistery

of it. His nephew Lorenzo was named Captain of the Army and his cousin Giuliano, Archbishop. In 1523, Giuliano also arrived at the Roman Papal seat under the name of Clement VII; he continued his predecessor's policy with the aid of the faithful Cardinal Passerini da Cortona. At the news of the Sack of Rome in 1527, the Florentine people revolted and once again drove out the Medici, or rather, their representatives. Following the alliance with Francis I, King of France, they prepared to endure the siege by the Spanish armies of Charles V. From the summer of 1529 to August 1530 the city resisted heroically. Finally, despite the sacrifice of the merchant Francesco Ferrucci who tried to free the city, Florence surrendered. With the loss of freedom, the singular political system ended too, and Florence became the capital of a dynastic state, similar to other Italian cities. The extraordinary cultural and artistic fecundity, during the political crisis, touched moments of great expressive tension with the two geniuses, Leonardo da Vinci (1452—1519) and Michelangelo (1475—1564), both interpreters, though in diametrically opposed ways, of a new social and spiritual condition.

Ponte Vecchio and Bridges

The Medici returned to Florence with the official title of Dukes. Alessandro, dissolute and overbearing, was killed by the dagger of his cousin Lorenzino, who saw himself as the liberator of the city, and with him the main branch of the family became extinct. He was succeeded by the descendant of a collateral branch, Cosimo I, son of Giovanni dalle Bande Nere, famous captain of adventure. He governed for 37 years and his rule was good. He extended it over almost all Tuscany, made himself respected by both Spain and France, and finally gained the title of Grand Duke. Under Cosimo I Florence knew a new period of peaceful splendour which continued with his brother, Ferdinando I. These conditions of well-being slowly weakened with the successors, Cosimo II and Ferdinando II.

The chosen architects of the Grand Dukes were successively Giorgio Vasari (1511—74), author among other things of a famous «Life of the Finest Painters, Sculptors and Architects», Bernardo Buontalenti (1536—1608) and Matteo Nigetti (1560—1649). It is important, however, that Florence in the XVI and partly in the XVII Cent. continued to exercise its vocation as a city of culture and that the Court of the Medici favoured

Uffizi Gallery. Leonardo da Vinci: Annunciation

and attracted scientists and artists of great note. The goldsmith and sculptor, Benvenuto Cellini (1500—71), historians and political writers such as Niccolò Machiavelli (1469—1527), Francesco Guicciardini (1483—1540), painters and sculptors such as Pontormo (1494—1557) and Giambologna (1524—1608), important scientists such as Galileo Galilei (1564—1642) and Evangelista Torricelli (1608—47).

Cosimo III, who ruled many years (he died in 1723), had the merit of maintaining a certain autonomy of front as regards the politics of the great European powers, but he was a man so strictly observant in religious matters as to skirt bigotry. The lively, spirited city of past centuries was going into a decline with its processions and religious functions while the Inquisition had a free hand in weaving plots of suspicion and fear. The Grand Duke's court no longer welcomed men of art and free spirits, but only intriguing priests and nuns; all civil life was reduced to a parody of the monastic. The successor Gian Gastone, a weak and dissolute man, faint-hearted and nearly always drunk, left no heirs and at his death the Grand Duchy of Tuscany passed to the Princes of Lorraine.

San Lorenzo, New Sacristy.
Michelangelo Buonarroti:
Night

San Lorenzo, New Sacristy.
Michelangelo Buonarroti:
Twilight

al of S. Maria del
Michelangelo
roti: Pietà

San Lorenzo, New Sacristy.
ichelangelo Buonarroti: Day

San Lorenzo, New Sacristy.
Michelangelo Buonarroti:
Dawn

PIAZZA DELLA SIGNORIA
SANTA CROCE

The political centre of the city of Florence is the Piazza della Signoria. Here, before being razed to the ground, rose the tower-houses of the Ghibelline, Farinata degli Uberti who opposed the destruction of the city after his party beat the Guelphs. The episode is recalled by Dante in The Inferno, where Farinata is placed within the circle of heretics. Here is the grandiose **Palazzo Vecchio,** so named after 1559 when Cosimo I abandoned it to install himself and his Court at the Pitti Palace. The severe fortified building is of the end of the XIII Cent. It was actually begun around 1298 and in 1314 was still under construction. Tradition gives the name of Arnolfo di Cambio as designer and builder, executing here one of the most significant examples of Italian public buildings. Above this compact but elegant pile, slender and agile rises the battlemented tower, called Arnolfo's Tower (94 metres high). The building was enlarged successively in the XVI Cent. by Vasari and Buontalenti. Previously Michelozzo Michelozzi, official architect to Cosimo the Elder, had renewed the arcaded courtyard, in a form by then clearly Renaissance, and the elaborate ceiling of the Hall of the Duecento, in carved panels by Benedetto da Maiano. Cronaca built the Great Hall of the Cinquecento midway through the XV Cent. These two great rooms served for meetings of the Great and Lesser Councils of the Florentine Republic. Later the palace was also the public dwelling place of the Signore and for that reason was embellished and decorated under the direction of Giorgio Vasari. A visit to the rooms reveals innumerable aspects of historic, literary and artistic thought in XVI Cent. Florence. The «Study» of Francesco I, the «Treasury» of Cosimo I are two charming little rooms created by Vasari as places of meditation and study for the two princes. The Monumental Apartments consist of a series of rooms whose decorative themes are linked with the lives of the best-known members of the Medici family. Leo X's Room, the Chapel, Clement VII's Room, that of Giovanni dalle Bande Nere, of Cosimo the Elder, of Lorenzo the Magnificent, of Cosimo I. On the Second Floor the Apartment of the Elements, prepared by the architect Battista del Tasso on behalf of Cosimo I who lived there from 1540. The name derives from the decoration which Vasari painted in the first room. In 1562 the same Vasari transformed the ancient apartment of the Priors, now destined to be the Apartment of the Duchess Eleonora of Toledo. The following rooms are the oldest ones, sober and austere and take us back to the times of the Republic and Savonarola; the Signoria Chapel, Audience Room (the ceiling and friezes are by the Da Maiano brothers), the Lily Room, so-called from the decoration in gold fleurs-de-lis on a blue field. In the Segreteria Niccolò Machiavelli had his office; the mother of Cosimo I, Maria Salviati, lived in the entresol. It is interesting to visit the Ballatoio, that is the fortified crowning of the palace from which one goes up to the Tower.

In Cosimo I's time there was an idea of transforming the entire Square and Michelangelo had suggested surrounding it with a continuous series of arcades like the Priors' Loggia; but because of the expense, the plan

Uffizi Gallery. Cleomenes of Apollodoros: the Medicean Venus

Uffizi Gallery. Sandro Botticelli: Birth of Venus

was not realized. On the left of the Palazzo Vecchio, from 1560 to 1575, Bartolomeo Ammannati erected the **Fountain of Neptune,** whose image in marble is surrounded by numerous allegorical statues in bronze. The architect availed himself of the collaboration of Giambologna, who is also responsible for the equestrian statue of Cosimo. The marble disk near the fountain indicates the point where Savonarola was hanged and burned.

On the right side rises the **Priors' Loggia** (of the Signoria), attributed to a project by Orcagna. The building, completed in 1382 served to accommodate the Signoria during public manifestations. Later it was occupied by the Ducal guard formed of Lansquenets, from which it took the name of Loggia dei Lanzi. Beneath the three wide arcades are now collected numerous statues, among which the most famous are the «Perseus», a masterpiece by Benvenuto Cellini (1554), and the «Rape of the Sabines» by Giambologna. Among the buildings around the Square, we remember the **Court of Commerce** of mid-XIV Cent. and the XVI Cent. **Uguccioni Mansion.** To house the administrative offices Cosimo I gave orders to Vasari to build an edifice on the right-hand side of the Palazzo Vecchio.

Giorgio V
Uffizi Cou

The **Palace of the Uffizi (Offices)** was built between 1560 and 1580; two long parallel arms, with arcade and loggia above, connected with the ducal residence by means of a passage. Later Cosimo I had a covered corridor built which, passing above Ponte Vecchio (the Old Bridge), joined the Pitti Palace. To-day it houses one of the most esteemed galleries in Italy and the world. The Picture Gallery gives an exhaustive and extremely rich panorama of Italian and also foreign painting, from its beginnings up to the XVIII Cent. The most famous and best-known canvases are «The Madonna in Majesty», Cimabue; «Madonna and Child», Giotto; the «Annunciation», Simone Martini; the «Adoration of the Magi», Gentile da Fabriano; the «Battle of San Romano», Paolo Uccello; the «Portraits of Federico da Montefeltro and Battista Sforza», Piero della Francesca; the «Birth of Venus», «Spring», and the «Madonna with the Pomegranate», Sandro Botticelli. And again, «The Adoration of the Magi» and the «Annunciation», Leonardo da Vinci; the «Allegory of Purgatory», Giovanni Bellini; the «Madonna with Goldfinch», and «Portrait of a Youth», L. Lotto; the «Old Rabbi», Rembrandt; the «Flora» and the «Venus with Lap-dog», Titian.

Piazza della Signoria: Costumed festivity

The Gallery also has Italian and Flemish tapestries, sculpture and miniatures from the XV to XVIII Cent. and the famous statue of the Medici Venus, (III Cent. B. C.), in addition to a Collection of prints and drawings.

Behind the Palazzo Vecchio opens the delightful S. Firenze Square, on to which face: in the corners the XV Cent. **Gondi Mansion,** the work of Giuliano da Sangallo, the **Convent of S. Firenze,** with the church of 1725 by Ruggeri. Closing the Square as it opens out into Via del Proconsolo, on one side is the group of buildings of the **Badia (Abbey)** on which rises a slender Gothic bell-tower, and on the other is the imposing pile of the **Bargello or Palace of the Podestà.** The front part with the Tower (the «Volognana») was built in 1255 as seat of the Captain of the People; in 1261 the Podestà lived there; later the Judges of the Rota Court; and from 1574 the Captain of Justice or Bargello, head of the police. Work went on around the palace up to half-way through the XIV Cent., the epoch in which rose the rear part around the beautiful arcaded courtyard with external stairway. The interior, for more than three centuries was continually being cut up and in some parts rebuilt to contain offices, and above all,

Bargello. Courtyard

prisons. It was destined in 1865 to become the seat of the National Museum, which houses a vast and important collection of Tuscan sculpture from XIV to XVII Cent.

In the entrance hall, large vaults on imposing pilasters, will be ordered the works by Michelangelo now in the museum. The highlights of this museum are to be seen in the work of Michelangelo, of Donatello and Verrocchio, in addition to a collection of goldsmiths' work, enamels, glass, wrought iron, bronzes and ivories, all of inestimable artistic value, and also wood statues of the XIV—XV Cent. Michelangelo is present with the «Drunken Bacchus», «Tondo with the Madonna and little St. John». «David», the splendid bust of «Brutus», and the «Martyrdom of St. Andrew». In the hall of the Great Council the works of Donatello: «St. George», the head of Niccolò da Uzzano, the «Davids» in bronze and in marble: «St. John Baptist», «St. Joachim», «Cupid», and «Attis». Other artists are Desiderio da Settignano, Michelozzo Michelozzi, Ghiberti, Bertoldo, Agostino di Duccio, the Vecchiettas, Luca della Robbia. In the Podestà's Chapel, where those condemned to death were assisted during their last hours, the frescoes in very bad state of preservation are attributed to Giotto.

National Museum or Bargello. Antonio del Pollaiolo: Bust of a Young Warrior

National Museum or Bargello. Desiderio da Settignano: Bust of a Youth

Piazza San Firenze: Towers of Bargello, Badia and Dome of S. Maria del Fiore

In one of them appears the portrait of Dante. There are certain master-pieces by Verrocchio, such as the polychrome terracotta of the «Resurrection», the «David» in marble, two «Madonnas», the «Portrait of Pietro di Lorenzo dei Medici», the «Gentlewoman with posy», the low relief of the «Death of Francesca Tornabuoni». On the 2nd Floor, by the sculptures of Cellini (Narcissus and the models for Perseus) we can see the terracottas of Andrea and Giovanni della Robbia, the «Bust of a Warrior» and «Hercules and Antaeus» by Pollaiolo, and again exceptional creations by Rossellino, Benedetto da Maiano, Mino da Fiesole, Laurana, Sansovino, Bernini, Riccio, etc.

The Medici Medal Collection is also interesting with examples of the work of Pisanello, Matteo dei Pasti, Michelozzo and Cellini.

In a side street to the right, **Dante Alighieri's House,** re-built and restored many times through the centuries, but which, nevertheless, tradition indicates as that in which the poet was born and lived. Facing is the Castagna Tower first residence of the Priory of the Arts.

The **Pazzi Mansion,** built by the powerful Florentine family who plotted against the Medici, is commonly attributed to Brunelleschi, while the fine

31

interior courtyard is the work of Giuliano da Maiano in 1472. The Anthropological Museum has found a home in the **Strozzi Mansion,** called the «Nonfinito» (Unfinished) because left unfinished by Bernardo Buontalenti.

From S. Firenze Square by Via d'Anguillara one crosses the so-called Via Torta (Crooked street), whose curvilinear course is due to the fact that the houses along it rise over the ancient Roman Amphitheatre, reaching the XIV Cent. **Peruzzi Mansion,** noticeable immediately because of its curved façade; one then arrives in the spacious Piazza Croce (Holy Cross Square), centre of religious and social life. In the XIV Cent. the Franciscans preached here, in the following century were held splendid festivals, tournaments, joustings, in which the nobility of Florence participated.

At the end, the **Church of Santa Croce (Holy Cross),** one of the best known Italian Gothic buildings. Begun towards the end of the XIII Cent. it was only completed a century later. While the façade on designs by Matas, and the bell-tower by Baccani are XIX Cent. works in neo-Gothic style, the interior of the church maintains the original structure, the project for which is attributed to Arnolfo di Cambio. In three naves, the central one

Basilica of S. Croce, Cloisters; and Tower and Bridge of San Niccolò

very wide, small transept and chapels aligned along the end, following the well known Egyptian Cross plan. The interior spaciousness is defined by architectonic lines of extreme essentiality, which though an expression of Gothic art, touch in their entirety a classical composure. The great popularity of the Franciscan Order induced rich and noble personages to request, in return for generous donations, the privilege of being buried in churches dedicated to St. Francis. In the Fourteenth Century the floor of Santa Croce was entirely covered with tombstones, the walls closely lined with funeral monuments, cenotaphs, commemorative plaques, and frescoes. After 1560 Vasari renewed the place, unfortunately raising the floor and doing away with the wall frescoes; he destroyed the choir, and placed the present altars against the walls. In spite of this, the works of art in Santa Croce are numerous and exceptional. On the 3rd pilaster to the right Benedetto da Maiano built the marble pulpit decorated with reliefs of a rare elegance. In the Bardi Chapel Giotto frescoed moving «Stories of St. Francis» and in the Peruzzi Chapel «Stories of the Baptist and St. John Evangelist». Taddeo Gaddi, a collaborator of Giotto himself, and Agnolo Gaddi frescoed the Main Chapel and the Castellani and Baroncelli Chapels.

Basilica of S. Croce. Interior

ca of S. Croce. Desiderio da Settignano:
ment to Carlo Marsuppini

Basilica of S. Croce. Bernardo Rossellino:
Tomb of Leonardo Bruni

In the fifth chapel to the left the frescoes representing «Stories of St. Sylvester» are the work of Maso di Banco. Among the numerous works of sculpture, we recall «The Annunciation», a delicate stone relief, and the «Crucifix» in wood, of great realism, both works by Donatello. The tomb of Leonardo Bruni, executed in 1444 by Rossellino, served as a model to all the Florentine artists of the XVI Cent. The Medici Chapel or Chapel of the Novitiate, was built by the architect Michelozzo for Cosimo the Elder in clear and well-balanced Renaissance form brightened by numerous Della Robbian terracottas. Among the numerous personalities who have been buried here, we recall the names of Michelangelo, Machiavelli, Galileo Galilei, Alfieri, Foscolo, Rossini.

From the Martello Door to the right of the façade one enters the XIV Cent. cloister, to which the **Pazzi Chapel** forms the background. Built between 1430—45 by Filippo Brunelleschi, it is a building on a central plan surmounted by the dome and preceded by an arcade with a huge central arch. Here the architect materialized his ideal of a religious building. The second cloister, known as the Great Cloister, was also planned by Brunelleschi shortly before his death, and decorated by Rossellino.

PIAZZA DEL DUOMO

From the Piazza della Signoria one gets to the Cathedral Square along Via Calzaiuoli, one of the main arteries of the city. On the left is one oft the most attractive Florentine Gothic buildings, **Orsanmichele,** built in 1337 as the Market Loggia for Grain. In the year 1380 the building was raised two floors opened by elegant double mullions, then consecrated and dedicated to the cult. The great Gothic triple mullions on the ground floor, designed by Talenti to close the arcades are very elaborate. The statues decorating the many niches of the pilasters are a veritable gallery of Florentine sculpture from the XIV to XVI Cent. Ghiberti produced «The Baptist», «St. Matthew» and «St. Stephen»; Verrocchio «The Doubting of Thomas»; by Giambologna is «St. Luke»; «St. Peter and the Princess» and «St. Mark» by Donatello. The other statues are by Nanni di Banco, Lombardi, Ferrucci and Baccio da Montelupo.

In the interior is preserved the Tabernacle by Andrea Orcagna (1349—59) who interpreted the Florentine Gothic taste with great richness of decoration, reliefs and mosaics.

In the Cathedral Square and that of S. Giovanni, which naturally follows it, rise two of the most famous city monuments, the Baptistery and the Church of S. Maria del Fiore.

The building of the **Baptistery,** in the minds of many critics goes back actually to the V Cent.; others consider it of the XII Cent. Probably the later building was superimposed upon and included a pre-existing temple. It is on an octagonal plan, with a series of pilasters in a double order which support the trabeation and the arcades on high. The dome is hidden on the exterior by a high XIII Cent. attic with a pyramidal roof. The façades are all covered with slabs of white and green marble which create a vivacious and elegant two-colour effect. The bronze doors of the three entrance Portals are exceptional. The oldest door is the work of Andrea Pisano (1336), in which is represented the «Story of the Life of St. John the Baptist» within lobated low-relief panels. Between 1403 and 1424 Lorenzo Ghiberti modelled the north door, and between 1425 and 1452 that facing the Cathedral, called the «Gate of Paradise», where by now Renaissance taste appears firmly established. In the interior of the building, which is of unusual vastness and majesty, the walls are covered with slabs of rare marble, while the architectonic part repeats the external scheme with pilasters and double mullioned loggias. The segmented dome is covered with mosaics composed on Byzantine lines by Venetian and Florentine workers in the XIII Cent.

The interest Florentines showed in St. John's Baptistery was always keen; even Dante often recalls it in his writings.

The people and the government had the same interest and possibly greater participation in the **Cathedral.** They wished it to be more imposing, larger and more sumptuous than any other Italian cathedral, particularly that of Pisa. But such pride was bound to bear the Florentines to an architectonic «impasse» from which they emerged only thanks to the genius of Brunelleschi. This artist's fame is justly linked with the solution of a problem which to his predecessors and contemporaries had proved impossible to resolve; the prob-

San Giovanni and Piazza Duomo.
try, Cathedral of S. Maria del Fiore, Giotto's Campanile

Piazza S. Giovanni, Baptistry
Lorenzo Ghiberti:
The Gate of Paradise

Creation of Adam and Eve
Original Sin
Expulsion from Paradise

Lorenzo Ghiberti:
Self-portrait

Sacrifice of Noah on leaving the Ark
The Drunkenness of Noah

Decorative motif

A Prophet

Birth of Esau and Jacob
Selling of the Birthright
Isaac orders Esau to go hunting
Rebekah counsels Jacob
Isaac's fraud

Artists
Mythical figures

Moses receiving the Tables
of the Law

War against the Philistines
Death of Goliath

Portrait of Vittorio Ghiberti, son of Lorenzo

The Trades of Mankind
Sacrifice of Cain and Abel
The Slaying of Abel
God rebukes Cain

Figure of a Saint

Decorative motif

Abraham kneeling before Angels
Sacrifice of Isaac

Portraits of Artists
Mythical figures

Joseph sold by his brothers
The finding of the Golden Cup
in Benjamin's Sack

The People of Israel in Jordan
Conquest of Jerico

Solomon and the Queen of Sheba

lem concerned the «dome» of the Cathedral. Brunelleschi's knowledge of the Gothic tradition and his studies of Roman building methods led him to develop a structure that the limits of traditional technique were unable to conceive. The Cathedral was begun in 1294 in a grandiose form on an original project worked out by Arnolfo di Cambio and then considerably amplified by the architect Francesco Talenti. Beyond the long arm of the crossing, the space becomes limited by the sides of an octagon, which measures about fifty-two metres in diameter. In 1410 the building of a drum, decided probably under the stress of emotional factors, aggravated the situation, carrying the height of the building to fifty-six metres. Brunelleschi did not lose heart and in the light of his studies carried out in Rome, he succeeded in finding the solution. Unlike the dome of the Pantheon, that of the Florentine Cathedral rested on far more fragile structures; it was impossible to find trees sufficiently long for the trusses. In an original combination of methods of construction and ancient and modern aesthetic principles, Brunelleschi selected the Gothic deep, curved vaulting ribs as the bearing element for the lesser lateral thrust and adapted the building method without centring to the use of elements

Ponte Vecchio: View towards Borgo San Jacopo

Via dello Studio

Cathedral Museum. Luca della Robbia: Singing Gallery (detail)

shaped in concentric circles of progressively diminishing diameter. The internal cavity, moreover, rendered the whole structure much lighter. In 1420 the building of the dome was begun, but ended only in 1436. The façade, left uncompleted, was finished in 1887; the interior, in three naves on pilasters and pointed arches is lit by large windows and by openings in the drum with stained glass windows designed respectively by Ghiberti, Donatello and Paolo Uccello. The lastnamed sculptor painted the fresco of the «Condottiere John Hawkwood».

Brunelleschi's enormous dome was frescoed by Vasari and Zuccari in 1579 with «The Last Judgment». In the first apsidal chapel is the unfinished «Pietà» by Michelangelo (1555). Behind the cathedral is the Cathedral Museum where are collected the sculptures coming from the early façade as well as the original panels of the **Bell Tower.**

This building rises isolated in the Square and is distinguished by the originality of its architectonic form, and for the richness of its decoration in polychrome marble. On the base are low reliefs by Andrea Pisano who collaborated with Giotto in the erection of the bell tower itself, begun in 1334 and continued in the upper floors by Talenti.

At one time the Church of **S. Lorenzo** rose outside the first circle of walls. Of very ancient foundation, it was, in fact, consecrated by Saint Ambrose, Bishop of Milan, in 393. It was re-built in Romanesque days and reconsecrated in 1060. In 1423 Giovanni di Bicci dei Medici gave the task of rebuilding it to Filippo Brunelleschi, who realized here his purest Renaissance work. He worked on it from 1425 to 1446; after his death, the work was continued on original designs by Antonio Manetti.

S. Lorenzo became virtually the family church of the Medici family. It was the Medici who entrusted to Michelangelo the task of building the interior façade, the New Sacristy and the Library, as well as the exterior façade which, however, was never accomplished. Later the Grand Dukes added the Chapel of the Princes. The interior is in three naves, with lacunar ceiling having a white background and gilded rosettes; along the sides is a continuous series of chapels. Among the numerous works of art the two Pulpits with bronze relief panels and the marble Choir by Donatello, the lovely Tabernacle by Desiderio da Settignano; the Annunciation by Filippo Lippi.

At the extreme left is the small area of the Old Sacristy, a jewel of Renais-

Church and Square of S. Lorenzo

sance architecture, the work of Brunelleschi (1420—29); the sculptural decoration in relief was executed by Donatello, who was also the sculptor of the appealing bust of «San Lorenzo» (St. Laurence) in terracotta, of the «Saints Cosmas and Damian» and of the bronze reliefs of the door.

In the beginning, the Medicean tombs were arranged in this Sacristy; the parents of Cosimo the Elder beneath the central floor panel, his sons, Giovanni and Pietro, in the stupendous porphyry and bronze sarcophagus conceived and constructed by Verrocchio together with Leonardo da Vinci. To contain the mortal remains of the other Medicis, the previously mentioned New Sacristy was built, a true chapel, with an independent entrance. How very elegant and serene is Brunelleschi's architectonic ideal, and how very dynamic and tragic that of Michelangelo. Buried here are Giuliano dei Medici, slain during the Pazzi plot, and Lorenzo the Magnificent; the other two sepulchres were completed by Michelangelo; the first is dedicated to Lorenzo, Duke of Urbino, whose statue in the centre shows him in an attitude of meditation (he was, in fact, known as «the thinker»). Reclining on the sarcophagus are the two symbolic figures of Dawn and Dusk; the second to Giuliano, Duke of Nemours, third child of Lorenzo the Magnif-

San Lorenzo Church. Interior

icent, who died at an early age. He is depicted by the sculptor wearing a cuirass and with the staff of command in his hand. At his feet are the two figures of Day and Night. These statues are justly considered among the masterpieces of Michelangelo for their dramatic and expressive power.

The monumental Chapel of the Princes, built by Nigetti in line with the apse of the church, is on an octagonal plan and its walls are panelled with precious marbles and hard stones of a dark colour, which lend a funereal aspect to the place. Buried in the crypt below are Cosimo I, Francesco I, Ferdinando I, Cosimo II, Ferdinando II, Cosimo III. From the Cloister in the style of Brunelleschi, one enters the Laurentian Library, built by Michelangelo, where are assembled codices and manuscripts of inestimable value. On the opposite part of the square rises the **Medici-Riccardi Mansion,** which faces the wide, straight Via Cavour, traced out in the time of Cosimo the Elder during the building of his private residence, begun in 1444 by Michelozzo Michelozzi. The scheme is that of Florentine mansions of the XV Cent., on a square plan with central courtyard and colonnade. The façades, the wall-facings of which become smoother and lighter

Via dei Cimatori   Via Vinegia

on every floor, are terminated on high by a bold cornice, and opened on the upper storeys by elegant double mullions arranged in a precise succession. In 1670 the new owners, the Riccardis, enlarged the building, throwing the perfect geometric figure of the building out of balance (the 10 original windows are those distinguished by the Medici escutcheon). In these rooms dwelt Cosimo's son, Pietro, and Lorenzo the Magnificent who here held his splendid court.

When Cosimo I moved to the Palazzo Vecchio, the magnificent decorations and furnishings were transported to the new seat, and then to the Uffizi. On the first floor there still remains, though damaged by the addition of the monumental Staircase, the Chapel conceived by Michelozzo and decorated by Benozzo Gozzoli with lovely frescoes depicting the Adoration of the Magi; a long, multi-coloured procession winds through the Tuscan countryside, while a host of angels hover in the sky above. Many of the figures represented here are portraits of the Medicis and of Italian princes. Of the present interior decoration, special attention is merited by the Gallery frescoed by Luca Giordano with the «Apotheosis of the Medici family».

The Arno, Santa Trínita Bridge and Ponte Vecchio

The three daughters of Piero the Gouty and Lucrezia Tornabuoni: **Maria, Lucrezia or Nannina, Bianca,** sisters of Lorenzo the Magnificent and Giuliano. Maria married Lionello de' Rossi, Bianca married Guglielmo dei Pazzi, and Lucrezia, Bernardo Rucellai, one of the most renowned scholars of the times.

John VIII Palaeologus, Emperor Constantinople attended the Coun in 1439. He was the last emperor b one prior to the fall of the Easte Roman Empire. As the successor Constantine the Great he was t greatest king on earth. When the fres was painted his empire had ceas to exist for 16 years.

...seph, Patriarch of Constantinople. He ...d come to Florence for the Council ...d died there. He is buried in the ...urch of S. Maria Novella.

Castruccio Castracani (1281-1328) of the Antelminelli, lord of Lucca and formidable enemy of Florence. He is shown here attempting to ride through a crowd of learned Florentines. His failure to do so shows that despite his power and that of his city, Florence, under the Medici rule, is now far above his reach and the most important city in Tuscany.

POSTQVAB CONSVMATI SVNT DIES OCTO VT CIRCVCIDERET͛ PVER VOCATV E NOM EͥꝐ IHESͥ.LVCE.II.C

ELONGAVI FVGIENS 7 MANSI INSOLITVDINE . P̄S . XXXXXV . C

SVRGE ACCIPE PVERVM 7 MATREM EͥꝐ 7 FVGE INEGIPTVM .MACEI.II.C

SAN MARCO, ACADEMY

Via Cavour, then known as Via Larga (the wide street), became during the years of Lorenzo dei Medici, one of the poles of city life. It ends in St. Mark's Square on to which look the **Convent** and **Church of St. Mark.** This complex rising in the centre of a green area of gardens and orchards dates from the end of the XII Cent. In 1437 Cosimo instructed his architect Michelozzo to rebuild it. The Monastery buildings were at that time re-built from the foundations, while the preexisting Romanesque-Gothic Church was only enlarged and restored. The façade was added in the second half of the XVIII Cent. in Baroque style. It is the first monastic building erected in Renaissance form, and it was the spiritual and cultural heart of Fifteenth Century Florence. To-day it houses the Museum of St. Mark or of Angelico. In fact, assembled here are almost all the pictorial works of Beato (Blessed).

From the Square, one enters at the right of the church: the first cloister is dedicated to St. Antoninus, prior of St. Mark's and then archbishop of the city. In agreement with Michelozzo, he entrusted the pictorial decoration to Angelico, following a project which proposed in some parts of the building, scenes of aesthetic subjects suited to remind the friars of the rules of their monastic life. The numerous stories depicted in the lunettes of this first cloister were painted later in the XVI Cent. and the first years of the XVII Cent. contrary to the prior's intention to leave most of the walls plain. Only 5 frescoes depicting

«St. Dominic at the foot of the Cross», «St. Thomas», «Christ and two Dominicans», «Pietà», and «St. Peter, Martyr» are by Angelico. On the right the rooms of the Pilgrims' Hostel where numerous panel paintings by Angelico are assembled, among them the Linaioli (Flax-Workers) «Madonna» (1433), a «Last Judgment» and 35 panels with «Stories of Jesus».

On the other side of the cloister, from the Hall of the Lavabo one reaches the Great Refectory. The large fresco at the end was executed by Sogliani, a follower of Fra Bartolomeo, painter of the «Last Judgment» in the same room. Fra Bartolomeo was the other great Dominican painter of St. Mark's (1475—1517); an ardent supporter of Savonarola, he donned the habit after the monk's death. In the Chapter Room where the friars used to confess their sins publicly and underwent punishment, Angelico painted the great allegorical fresco of the «Crucifixion». In the Small Refectory Domenico Ghirlandaio frescoed a great «Cena» (Supper) (1480 c.).

Now one goes into the second Cloister, of Saint Dominic, planned by Michelozzo. On the first floor where the little cells of the friars follow one another in single or double rows along three sides, Angelico, between 1439 and 1445, frescoed in each of these episodes from the life of Christ and of the Madonna. He was helped by several pupils among whom was Benozzo Gozzoli. At the top of the stairs is an Annunciation of considerable poesy. Facing the cell of St. Antoninus, at the end of the same corridor are two cells reserved for Cosimo the Elder as a retreat, decorated with a Crucifix and with the Adoration of the Magi. Now we are at the entrance to the Library, planned by Michelozzo in obvious

rk's Museum. Beato Angelico: Flight into Egypt

Renaissance form, with three naves on columns (1441). Here are assembled eight hundred precious volumes collected by the Humanist Niccolò Niccoli who thus spent all his substance. He donated them to the monastery so that they might remain at the disposition of scholars, in the manner of modern public libraries. In the second corridor the fresco of the «Madonna Enthroned» and in the cells «The Annunciation», the «Transfiguration», the «Marys at the Sepulchre», «The Coronation», the «Presentation at the Temple» and others as well. At the end of the third corridor are the Prior's Quarters which at the end of the XV Cent. were occupied by Savonarola. They consist of three small rooms where are now assembled iconographic documents of the preacher-reformer friar, among them the portrait by Fra Bartolomeo. In the first cloister is preserved the bell called the «Piagnona» (Wailer) which called the people to listen to Savonarola's preaching and which was torn down by the Medici partisans from the bell tower and symbolically whipped through the streets of the city. The adjacent church of St. Mark's was re-built internally by Giambologna and Silvani, in 1580 and 1678 respectively. Giambologna planned Saint Antoninus' Chapel, where is preserved the saint's body, transferred at the end of the XVI Cent.

St. Mark's Church and Square

St. Mark's Museum. Beato Angelico: Deposition

from the Sacristy (Michelozzo). The frescoes on the walls in fact portray the ceremony of the transfer and were carried out by Domenico Crespi il Passignano; the other paintings and sculpture provide a review of the taste of Florentine artists of the end of the XVI Cent. At the corner of Via degli Arazzieri is the **Little Mansion of Livia,** built by Bernardo Fallani, on behalf of the Grand Duke Pietro Leopoldo who assigned it to the dancer Livia Malfatti. Adjacent to St. Mark's Square, the **Academy Gallery** houses a group of splendid sculptures by Michelangelo, among them the statue of «David», and the roughed out statues of the «Slaves» which were to decorate the Tomb of Pope Julius II. These figures of extreme power and drama seem to emerge arrogantly from the marble, freeing themselves by their own strength from the inanimate material. In the Picture Gallery are paintings of the Tuscan and Florentine schools: Gaddi, Jacopo di Cione, Spinello Aretino, Baldovinetti, Paolo Uccello, Botticelli, Lippi, Ghirlandaio, Raphael.

The **Refectory of St. Apollonia,** refectory of the ancient monastery of the same name, preserves the wonderful fresco by Andrea del Castagno depicting «The Last Supper», one of the most renowned works of the Renais-

er of Palazzo della
oria, Dome of S. Maria
Fiore, Giotto's
panile

sance and the artist's masterpiece; in addition, by the same artist, a Crucifixion, Deposition and Resurrection and the series of Portraits, detached from the Villa of Legnaia (Dante, Petrarch, Boccaccio, Farinata degli Uberti, Pippo Spano, Niccolò Acciaioli). Many other interesting buildings rise in the area where there was once the great Garden of St. Mark's. Here Lorenzo the Magnificent had assembled innumerable ancient statues and low-reliefs bought in Rome.

Coming back to the buildings still existing, particular mention should be made of the **Medici Country House,** built by Buontalenti in solemn XVI Cent. form on behalf of the Grand Duke Francesco I; the **Cloister of the Scalzi** of the early XVI Century decorated by Andrea del Sarto with chiaroscuro frescoes depict «Stories of John the Baptist»; the **Pandolfini Mansion** built by the Sangallo brothers it seems on drawings by Raphael; the Bonifacio Hospital, founded in 1377 by the podestà Bonifacio Lupi, and destined after the passage of the armies of Charles VIII, to those suffering from «mal francese» (venereal disease). In 1788 Pietro Leopoldo ordered that mental patients should be housed and treated here, an exceptional arrangement for the period, while with a similarly enlightened spirit the doctor

Cenacle of S. Apollonia. Andrea del Castagno: Last Supper

Vincenzo Chiarugi created here the first psychiatric centre. At the corner between Via degli Alfani and Via dei Servi, rises Brunelleschi's **Rotonda,** a chapel commissioned by the Calimala merchants in 1434. Despite its incomplete state, and the ravages of time, thanks to recent restorations, the Rotonda presents a planimetric scheme that is both original and unique in Italy; an octagonal polygon in the interior which doubles the number of its sides externally. Not far away opens the loveliest of Florentine Renaissance squares, that of the Santissima Annunziata, perfectly square in form. Looking onto it is the **Foundling Hospital,** planned by Brunelleschi in the third decade of the century, with a long, low façade, opened by a graceful colonnade of nine slender arches. These were decorated on the spandrels with enamelled terracotta roundels by Andrea della Robbia and represent the now famous baby in swaddling clothes in memory of those abandoned and brought up here by the Florentine Republic. Internally, the building opens on to a fine arcaded courtyard, while some rooms house a gallery with works by Domenico Ghirlandaio, Pietro di Cosimo, Botticelli (an attribution), and Luca della Robbia; Bernardino Poccetti was the painter of the frescoes. Opposite the Foundling Hospital, Antonio da

St. Mark's Convent. Cloister

Sangallo the Elder and Baccio d'Agnolo erected the **Colonnade of the Confraternity of Servants of Mary** (1516). The third side was completed as a harmonic unit by Caccini towards 1600 with a Colonnade and by Ammannati with the **Grifoni Mansion** (1563). At the end of the Square rises the **Church of the SS. Annunziata,** the most famous sanctuary in Florence. Founded in the XIII Cent. it was re-built in the XV Cent., on drawings by Michelozzo, by Antonio Manetti and in the following centuries considerably transformed and damaged owing to external and internal additions. After a Baroque portico one enters the Cloister of the Vows, added by Manetti on a drawing by Michelozzo. The enlargement was made necessary by the great number of votive objects offered by the Florentines, among them richly clad, life-size wax statues of the most important personages, popes, monarchial lords (in 1630 the statues numbered over 600 in addition to 25,000 shields and panels). Today, the interior preserves the pompous XVII Cent. aspect with the exception of the marble Tempietto which contains the image of the Annunciation (Michelozzo). The most beautiful frescoes are those by Andrea del Sarto and Andrea del Castagno. In the adjacent Via della Colonna is the **Archaeological Museum.**

Piazza SS. Annunziata

55

P.ZA D. REPUBBLICA   VIA CAVOUR   VIA PÔR S. MARIA   PONTE VECCHIO   PASSETTO   PALAZZO
PAL. MEDICI-RICCARDI   VIA GUICCIARDINI   BASILICA DI S. MARIA DEL FIORE   VIA DEI BARDI   DELLA SIGNORIA

OLTRARNO, LEFT BANK

From the Piazza della Signoria one quickly arrives at the Arno where the two banks are joined by the **Ponte Vecchio** (Old Bridge), the ancient road junction at the foot of Fiesole which linked northern and southern Etruria. It is one of the most characteristic and well-known structures in Florence, built in 1345 by Neri di Fioravanti in stone on an earlier wooden construction. Shortly afterwards, under the lateral arcades, rose the shops let to meat retailers; at the beginning of the Sixteenth Century a government decree established that in these shops only goldsmiths and jewellers might stay. The external, projecting parts were then added so as to enlarge the internal space. Then Giorgio Vasari added, above the upstream shops, the corridor connecting the Uffizi with the Pitti Palace. Crossing to the other side of the river along Via Guicciardini, one arrives in front of the grandiose **Pitti Palace,** built by one of the most powerful merchant families in Florence, dreaded business rivals of the Medici themselves. Luca Pitti entrusted the plan to Brunelleschi in the year 1440, but the building was begun only in 1458 under the direction of Luca Fancelli. It was the wish of the owner that his mansion should be greater and more monumental than all the others then existing in the city, and in particular the Medici Mansion (the first floor windows had to be at least as large as the doors of the Medici). The fact is that the original nucleus is only that which to-day corresponds to the central part of the mansion with its seven windows.

Work was interrupted after eight years on account of the diminished economic resources of the family exhausted by political and mercantile rivalry. In 1549 Buonaccorso Pitti sold the mansion to the wife of Cosimo I, Eleonora of Toledo. Building was resumed in 1560 by Ammannati with the arrangement of the enormous courtyard and in the XVII Cent. by Giulio and Alfonso Parigi who lengthened the façade. The urban and structural arrangement of the complex is completed by two lateral wings at right angles to the façade, which is covered with rustication becoming smoother towards the top, rugged and severe compared with the grandeur of the rooms inside. For about three centuries the princely life of the Grand Dukes took place in these rooms, since they wished to have a seat worthy of their rank. The luxurious decoration was carried out for the entire duration of the Grand Duchy, and done with a singleness of purpose and intent despite the gradual and almost imperceptible variation of artistic taste. To-day it houses the Palatine Gallery, the Silver Museum, and the Gallery of Modern Art. The first collection, arranged by Ferdinando II with the principal nucleus in works inherited from his wife Vittoria della Rovere of Urbino, was then enriched by the Medicis and the Lorenas. Raphael is here with «The Pregnant Woman», the «Grand Duke's Madonna», the «Madonna of the Chair», Portraits of Angelo and Maddalena Doni: «The Veiled Woman», this last a portrait of the famous Fornarina, the painter's model whom he loved tenderly; Andrea del Sarto with «The Assumption», «St. John the Baptist», «The Annunciation» and «The Deposition».

A group of works of great beauty by Titian are assembled here: the «Portraits» of Philip II of Spain, of Cardinal Ippolito dei Medici, of Pietro Aretino, and in addition «The Magdalene», «The Englishman», «La Bella», «The Concert».

Behind the mansion extends the **Boboli Garden,** designed by Tribolo in 1550. In this stretch of green, made even more attractive by the nature of the hilly ground, rich in avenues, fountains, statues, pavilions, are held the interesting spectacles of the Florentine Musical May.

Above the garden, the **Belvedere Fortress,** erected in the last years of the XVI Cent. by the architect Buontalenti. From the Pitti Palace, passing in front of **Bianca Cappello's House,** the Venetian love of Francesco dei Medici, one arrives at the **Church of the Spirito Santo.** One of the most significant expressions of the early Florentine Renaissance, it was begun in 1444 by Brunelleschi and continued by Manetti, who followed the original design only in part. The annexed Augustinian convent had libraries, schools, pilgrims' hostels, refectories for the poor and a hospital. Founded in mid-XIII Cent. it was enlarged and developed to a point where it assumed great social and cultural importance. The very simple and partly ruined exterior of the church gives no hint of the refined and elegant beauty of the interior, planimetrically a Latin cross but with a slender colonnade

Bòboli Garden. Artichoke Fountain

Pitti Palace
Palatine Gallery. Raphael Sanzio: Madonna of the Grand Duke ▶

which continues on into the two arms of the transept and to the presbytery; along all sides open a continuous series of 40 chapels, decorated with sculptures by Rossellino, Sansovino and paintings by Filippino Lippi, Ghirlandaio and Botticelli. The Sacristy, on an octagonal plan, was conceived by Giuliano da Sangallo. The two cloisters were built respectively by Ammannati and Giulio Parigi; the only place remaining of the XIV Cent. convent is the spacious Refectory.

Another great building complex on this side of the Arno is that of the Convent of **St. Mary of the Carmine;** the Church of medieval origin was rebuilt in 1771 after a serious fire; saved from destruction was the Brancacci Chapel, the decoration on the walls of which constitutes convincing evidence of the glory of Italian painting.

It was begun by the late Gothic painter Masolino da Panicale, commissioned by the merchant, Felice Brancacci, continued by Masaccio around 1425 and completed by Filippino Lippi between 1474 and 1485. Masaccio, one of the greatest geniuses of Italian art, died in Rome at an early age, and under mysterious circumstances. He took up Giotto's message and carried it to its extreme consequences through the filter of the new Renaissance

Carmine Church and Square

◀ Palatine Gallery. Titian Vecellio: Portrait of a Gentleman or «The Englishman»

experiences. The dynamic power, the expressiveness, the colour, line and perspective express in absolute unity of style and concept the fulness of a humanity taken back to the palpitating moment of the creation. The themes are those of Original Sin, and of the Life of St. Peter. Upper order, left to right: Masaccio, «Expulsion from Paradise»; Masaccio, «Payment of Tribute Money»; Masolino, «Preaching of St. Peter»; Masaccio, «St. Peter baptising»; Masaccio, «St. Peter cures the Cripple»; Masolino, «Saint Peter Resuscitates Tabitha»; Masolino, «Temptation of Adam and Eve». Lower order: Lippi, «St. Peter visited in prison by St. Paul»; Masaccio and Lippi, «Saint Peter Resuscitates the son of Theophilus»; Masaccio, «St. Peter in the pulpit»; Masaccio, «St. Peter heals the sick»; Masaccio, «St. Peter and St. John give alms»; Lippi, «Condemnation of St. Peter» and «Crucifixion»; the last panel and the two lunettes were frescoed in XVIII Cent. by Meucci and Sacconi.

Before re-crossing the Arno by the S. Trínita Bridge let us recall the XIII Cent. Frescobaldi Mansion where in 1301 stayed Charles of Valois and his court.

Church of the Carmine, Brancacci Chapel. Masaccio: The Payment of Tribute Money

SANTA MARIA NOVELLA

At the foot of the S. Trínita Bridge, on the right, the **Ferroni Mansion,** severe grandiose building of the end of the XIII Cent of four storeys and crowned with corbelled battlements. Facing it, smaller but more elegant, is the **Gianfigliazzi Mansion,** it, too of XIII Cent. The Square is dominated by the **Church of Santa Trínita,** a significant example of Florentine Gothic architecture, built in the second half of the XIII Cent. The façade is a work of the end of the XVI Cent. by Buontalenti who already reflects the new Baroque taste. The interior, which is wholly preserved, is attributed to a plan by Nicola Pisano. Domenico Ghirlandaio frescoed the Sassetti Chapel between 1483 and 1491 with «Episodes from the Life of St. Francis»; some of them are set in the Florence of the time and very interesting are the figures of the donors and of the Medici. By the same painter is the Altar-piece with: «The Adoration of the Shepherds». In the second Chapel to the left of the choir is the tomb of Benozzo Federici, bishop of Fiesole, constructed in marble and in enamelled terracotta by Luca della Robbia. The column placed in the centre of the square comes from the Baths of Caracalla in Rome. On the right, towards the Piazza della Signoria are some characteristic streets leading to the ancient **Church of the Santi Apostoli,** in Romanesque style, built on a wall of the nearby Roman Baths and over the area of a children's cemetery. The beautiful **Davanzati Mansion** is a classic example of a XIV Cent. private residence with a narrow, very tall façade surmounted by an architraved loggia. The more peaceful city life at that time allowed of building walls broken by wide windows and portals on the ground floor. The interior courtyard lights the rooms facing along its sides, and the room known as «madornale» (huge) on the first floor assumes the character of a formal reception hall. The decoration is preserved almost intact both on the first floor and the second (among others the Parrot Room is famous). It now houses the Museum of Interior Decoration with Florentine furniture and furnishings of the XV and XVI Cent. One leaps backward a century looking at the **Tower Houses of the Foresi,** one of the most powerful factions of the city; much developed in height. Its narrow rooms inside receive little light from the small loophole windows. On the façade are the brackets which once supported the wooden bridges thrown from one house to another for communication when the streets were dangerous during rises and struggles between factions. The **Guelph Mansion** has a XIV Cent. façade; the opposite façade was rebuilt in the XV Cent. to a design by Brunelleschi and completed by Vasari later. Not far away is the **Loggia of the New Market,** built by Tasso towards the middle of the XVI Cent. Returning to Via dei Tornabuoni we arrive before one of the most interesting civic buildings of the XV Century, the **Strozzi Mansion,** begun in 1489 by Benedetto da Maiano and completed by Cronaca, with the rich, boldly projecting cornice and the internal courtyard galleried in two orders. From the surrounding bench the building develops on three floors, the ground one more secure, with very high square windows and with rougher, bolder rustication; the upper ones opened by a continuous series of arched

h of the Carmine, Brancacci Chapel. Masaccio: Expulsion from Paradise

Via Tornabuoni

double mullions resting on a string course of basic lines. The masonry, too, becomes smoother and less projecting toward the top.

In Via della Vigna Nuova, the **Rucellai Mansion,** another Renaissance building erected between 1446 and 1451 by Rossellino on a plan by Leon Battista Alberti. The architectonic and stylistic motifs of those years are repeated, but here greater grace and harmony are achieved apart from the greater regularity and less bold rustication, by the light attached pilasters rhythmically stressing the spaces between the windows. After the XVI Cent. **Larderel Mansion** by the architect Antonio Dosio, we enter Antinori Square. Here rises the Antinori mansion, attributed to Giuliano da Sangallo, and named after a family of silk merchants who bought the building from the Martellis in 1490. The **Church of S. Gaetano** which looks on to the square and originally of the XI Century was re-built in Baroque style towards the middle of the XVII Cent. by Matteo Nigetti. Another magnificent monument in this rapid itinerary is seen in the **Church of Santa Maria Novella** and the annexed convent. The Dominicans established themselves in this area in 1221, beginning the construction of their Florentine seat. The name New («Novella») is due to the fact that in 1279 the building structure was

Piazza S. Maria N
Church and Clo

renewed on the much more modest pre-existing one. The two friar architects Sisto da Firenze and Ristoro da Campi began the building of the church, which then turned out to be the largest of their Order, in Romanesque-Gothic form; it was only completed two centuries later, between 1450 and 1470 on the plans of Leon Battista Alberti.

The lateral volutes of the upper part of the façade, panelled entirely in polychrome marbles, constitute the connection between the central nave and the lateral ones, and are seen here for the first time. The interior, in three naves on grouped pilasters and Gothic arches, marks an important moment in Italian Gothic architecture. Numerous art treasures are preserved here, beginning with Masaccio's stupendous fresco on the wall to the left corresponding to the third span, representing «The Trinity» (1428). The Choir is decorated with frescoes by Ghirlandaio representing «Episodes in the life of the Virgin and of St. John the Baptist». At the head of the transept opens the Rucellai Chapel with remains of XIV Cent. frescoes. The Filippo Strozzi Chapel, first on the right of the presbytery, is decorated by one of the last works of Filippino Lippi (1503), scenographic frescoes of «Stories of St. Philip and St. John the Baptist»; the Strozzi

Church of S. Maria Novella. Cloister

Tomb behind the altar was conceived by Benedetto da Maiano (end of XV Cent.). The famous Crucifix which Brunelleschi modelled in competition with Donatello is in the Gondi Chapel, planned by Giuliano da Sangallo in 1503. The only Chapel entirely preserved is that of the Strozzis of Mantua, decorated with marvellous frescoes by Nardo di Cione, called l'Orcagna, in 1357. On the end wall the «Last Judgment», on the right «Hell», and facing it «Paradise», with episodes inspired by the Divine Comedy of Dante, whose portrait appears among the figures of the blessed. The Altar Piece with «Jesus Christ Triumphant», is by the same artist.

Going into the Sacristy, built following the drawings of Jacopo Talenti one may admire there a Crucifixion attributed to Giotto and a marble lavabo inside a terracotta niche by Giovanni della Robbia.

One leaves the church to go into the Cloisters of the annexed monastery, a gothic complex of considerable interest. The Green Cloister, built in 1350, derives its actual name from the frescoes in green earth executed by various artists, among them Paolo Uccello (they are to-day displayed in the Refectory Room). On to this cloister opens the huge, famous Spanish Chapel, built by Talenti in 1359 for meetings of the Chapter of the Order.

Piazza del Duomo. «Scoppio del Carro»

When the Grand Duchess Eleonora of Toledo, wife of Cosimo I, assigned the chapel to the gentlemen of her retinue, it was indicated with the new denomination «the Spanish». The walls were entirely frescoed around 1367 by numerous Gothic painters, among whom was Andrea di Bonaiuto: on the end wall are Episodes from the Passion of Christ; on the right, Allegory of the Church militant and triumphant; on the left the Triumph of Wisdom; on the entrance wall «Stories of St. Peter».

The little Cloister of the Dead, of the Romanesque epoch, is very rich in tombs and sepulchres; the Great Cloister follows with a good fifty-one arches frescoed in the XVI and XVII Cent. (Carabinieri School). Again let us recall briefly the **Church of Ognissanti,** rebuilt in XVII Cent., which preserves in its interior frescoes by D. Ghirlandaio and Sandro Botticelli.

A type of building often repeated in Florence is the Loggia, which used to rise in the immediate vicinity of the mansion of the great lord. Beneath its arches were held family festivals on the occasion of births and marriages, the funerals of relatives were conducted with great solemnity, friends or clients met to attend horse tournaments or spectacles of other kinds. The people gathered there receiving food and drink lavished by the lord.

an Niccolò Tower

Sdrucciolo Pitti

PIAZZALE MICHELANGELO AND SURROUNDINGS

Taking as point of reference the Bridge called Alle Grazie, we re-cross the Arno and come to Mozzi Square, called after a family of bankers, on to which look the two **Torrigiani Mansions** built by Baccio and Domenico d'Agnolo. On the right is Via dei Bardi, which leads behind the Lungarno (River Bank) to the Ponte Vecchio, and is lined with fine mansions and houses. In Via San Nicolò, the Church of the same name founded in 1164 but many times re-built, Michelangelo found refuge in the bell-tower when fearing reprisals after the 1530 siege. Behind the XVI Cent. **Torrigiani Mansion** lived the Commander of the Florentine army during the same siege, Malatesta Baglioni.

The roads which rise to S. Miniato are numerous, wide and easy like Viale dei Colli (Avenue of the Hills) and Viale Michelangelo, or steeper and shorter like the ramps and steps flanked by rows of cypresses. Finally, between gardens and villas opens Piazzale (the Great Square) Michelangelo, perhaps the ideal spot from which to admire Florence stretching along the two banks of the Arno. The arrangement of this square is a work of the XIX Century. The **Church of San Salvatore al Monte,** surrounded by cypresses, was built by Cronaca in 1475 on the site of an ancient oratory.

By a final interesting flight of steps one goes up to the **Church of San Miniato al Monte,** a typical example of Florentine Romanesque art. Its simple and splendid marble covered façade is characterized by a precise and elegant geometrical design which underlines the extremely essential architectonic line. The church was begun in 1018 by Bishop Hildebrand and dedicated to St. Miniatus, a Christian martyr of the III Cent. who, according to legend, after being beheaded took his own head in his hands and, having climbed the hill, died on the spot where the church now stands, at that time a Christian cemetery. The building was finished only in the XIII Cent. The interior is in three naves with an open beamed roof and inlaid marble floor (1207). The presbytery is raised above the huge crypt. The latter with its seven naves and forest of slender, elegant columns was once frescoed on the walls (today only a few scraps remain, attributed to Taddeo Gaddi). Many artistic treasures enriched the church throughout various centuries. The lovely transennas and the sculptured inlaid Pulpit are of the early XIII Century; the wooden Choir is of the middle of the XV Cent. In the bowl of the apse is the huge mosaic of 1297 representing «Christ Blessing between Mary and St. Miniatus»; in the centre of the Church is the Tabernacle of the Crucifix designed by Michelozzo and decorated in the enamelled vault by Luca della Robbia. This work was ordered by Pietro dei Medici in honour of Giovanni Gualberto, founder of the Order of the Vallombrosians and one of the principal Florentine saints.

In the left-hand nave is the Chapel of the Cardinal of Portugal, a Renaissance work carried out with the collaboration of Antonio Manetti, who conceived the architectonic project, Luca della Robbia, who was responsible for the five tondi, Antonio Rossellino, who designed the sarcophagus, Antonio del

Pollaiolo, Alessio Baldovinetti and Pietro del Pollaiolo, the artists of the various paintings.

Through the Sacristy, frescoed by Spinello Aretino with «Stories of the life of St. Benedict», in 1387, one reaches the Cloister. Here in the upper gallery are remains of frescoes by Paolo Uccello. The Bell Tower, built in 1523 by Baccio d'Agnolo, still bears the signs of artillery fire during the siege of Florence. Next to the church, the **Bishops' Palace,** a Fourteenth Century battlemented building.

The hills form a crown to this beautiful city: the serene, gentle landscape had a great deal to do with the formation of the character of its inhabitants. After the monuments of the city it seems only natural to tour the surroundings of Florence where the green of the grass and the tillage is broken up by the silver green of olive trees and the dark green of the slender cypresses. Hamlets on the hilltops face each other over pleasant valleys, little roads wind up and down the slopes, at times open to broad panoramas, at others closed within low walls. Farmhouses and villas dot the area. Rapidly indicated here are some of these villages and centres which were often significant in the history of Florence.

Florence from Piazzale Michelangelo

Fiesole

The **Villa of Poggio Imperiale** was the luxurious country home of the Medici Grand Duchesses. Its present aspect goes back to the last years of the XVIII Cent. under Leopold I. Construction of the **Charterhouse of Galluzzo** was begun in 1341 at the expense of Niccolò Acciaioli who intended it for the Carthusians. Another religious centre rose in 1350 at Monte Oliveto. And here we are at last at **FIESOLE** with Etruscan and Roman remains; of the medieval city we remember the **Fiesolan Abbey** with a Romanesque façade contemporary with San Miniato, and a Renaissance interior; the imposing Romanesque **Cathedral** of 1028 and the battlemented Bell Tower; on top of the hill, where stood the ancient Acropolis, the **Convent of St. Francis** from which one dominates the entire panorama of the valley of Florence. From here one can reach the village of **SETTIGNANO.** The villas around Florence are nearly all associated with the Medici family who had them built and used them as summer or hunting residences: The **Medici Villa of Careggi,** re-built and fortified by Michelozzo in 1433. Here lived and died Cosimo the Elder and Lorenzo the Magnificent; the latter entertained men of letters and artists during the periods of his stay; **Villa di Castello,** where Giovanni, called «dalle Bande Nere» (of the Black Bands) spent

Villa Petraia

his youth, as did his son Cosimo, Grand Duke of Florence, and where
Francesco I held his splendid court; **Villa of the Petraia,** already celebrated
for having in 1364 resisted the assaults of the soldiers of John Hawkwood,
was bought by Cardinal Ferdinando dei Medici who had it completely re-
built in 1575 by Buontalenti; **Villa Salviati,** built in 1470 by Giuliano da
Sangallo; **Villa Palmieri** which tradition indicates as the place chosen by
Boccaccio for the setting of his Decameron; the **Medici Villa di Belcanto,**
built by Michelozzo in 1458 to the order of Cosimo the Elder (only a few
traces remain), celebrated for having been the home of the «Platonic
Academy», founded by Marsilio Ficino. With the **Villa of Poggio a Caiano**
Giuliano da Sangallo (about 1480) produced the model of the princely
country residence. In the great Hall of Honour the barrel vault is decorated
with frescoes of allegorical themes extolling the Medici family. Lorenzo
the Magnificent held his court there in spring. Here dwelt Pope Leo X, the
Emperor Charles V and the Archduchess Giovanna. In addition, Francis I
dei Medici and the Venetian Bianca Cappello died here almost contempo-
raneously, it is suspected of poisoning, in 1587; Cosimo III banished his
wife Louise of Orleans to these rooms prior to sending her back to France.

INDEX

INDEX OF ARTISTS AND THEIR WORKS

La Certosa

Tuscan countryside

BASILICA S. MARIA DEL FIORE

BATTISTERO

PALAZZO STROZZI   LUNG

PìAZZA INDIPENDENZA   PIAZZA